MAINTAINING BALANCE in a WOBBLY WORLD

Dr. Sheran Mattson

Copyright © 2014 Sheran Mattson

All Rights Reserved.

No part of this work may be reproduced by any means without the express written permission of the author.

Year of the Book Press
135 Glen Avenue
Glen Rock, PA 17327

ISBN 13: 978-1-942430-00-1

ISBN 10: 1-942430-00-0

About the Author

Dr. Sheran Mattson | Dynamic Life Coach

I help you create powerful relationships, both personally and professionally. With over 30 years' experience, I can help you through delicate life transitions as you seek to improve and grow.

Life can seem out of control at times. So many demands, so "little" time and so many expectations! I help you cultivate more peace and joy in your life.

Dr. Sheran Mattson holds a Doctoral degree in Spiritual Psychology, and Master's and Bachelor's degrees in Religious Studies and Early Childhood Education. She is ACEP EFT Certified with training in Hado Healing, Pranic Healing and Dahn Healing. She also has graduate studies in Counseling and Organizational Management. With over seventeen years as a Career Coach, Facilitator and Training, Dr. Mattson understands how to effectively create and support powerful relationships both personally and professionally.

About this Guide

We can feel alone in our struggle for positive change. We look around and it appears others have it all together!

What's amazing though is that we are all more alike than different. Most of us stay in a comfort zone with how our life progresses… even if we're not totally satisfied and would secretly like things to change.

When prompted to change by an outside force, we take steps we may have thought about but were too complacent to initiate on our own.

When I was a career coach working with people who were laid off from their jobs, I saw this firsthand. At first they could not imagine how they were going to survive. The world turned upside down. Eventually they realized a life altering event was just what they needed to make changes they'd been thinking about for a long time.

This workbook provides simple and practical ideas to use immediately so you can be more peaceful and have more joy in the *now*, without waiting for an external "kick in the pants."

These simple tools have worked for the many magnificent people I've coached. You also can enjoy the benefits of achieving *Balance in a Wobbly World*. Many suggestions in the following pages are simple reminders, many you may already know but have forgotten. Sometimes the simplest action makes the biggest impact! It's *using the tools* that makes the difference!

I would value hearing how you experience the ideas within these pages. Leave me a comment on the website www.sheranmattson.com or email me at sheran@dynamiclifecoach.net. When you're ready to implement even more balance I'm available for coaching by face to face, phone, or Skype.

> May you have Joy, Peace, and Balance in abundance!

Table of Contents

The 5 P's 1

What Am I Balancing? 5

Plan 13

Prioritize 21

Play 33

Positivity 41

Pick Your Yeses 49

The 5 P's

We live in a world of movement!

When was the last time you had absolutely nothing to do, nowhere to be with no expectations and no noise around you? If this happens for you often then read no further. You should write the best seller book on how you achieved that!

Our lives are driven by the demands of the many roles we play and the expectation we place on ourselves to perfectly meet each requirement. We are spouses, parents, employees, employers, caretakers, officers, volunteers and friends. Each role has its own set of activities, responsibilities, and commitments. When we begin the day, we may already feel behind on what needs to be done and accomplished. How do you decide what's most important—especially when tasks, dates, and places to be, all overlap?

With our many obligations, it is possible to lose the joy of the present moment. We drift to the past, filled with regret for what we didn't do – or should have done. We live in the future, immersed in a chore list of all the things we have not yet done or still must do.

There never seems to be enough time to finish all the things which seem so important or critical. You don't want to disappoint anyone,

> *When was the last time you had absolutely NOTHING to do?*

so you say "Yes" to everyone else's demands first. Your energy is scattered in too many directions. Then you end up disappointing yourself.

Do you get depleted and do whatever you can to fill up again? The balance you so desire seems out of reach and unrealistic. Coffee doesn't help and neither does chocolate!

The best thing you can do is to avoid imbalance in the first place. It is unrealistic to think you're going to give up the roles you love or have chosen. The next best thing is to practice behaviors that allow you to stay present and flow with whatever shows up. You can take simple steps and use effective and proven tools to release the effects of stress. These techniques allow self-sabotaging beliefs to surface and be released. You are able to clean out old messages that have lingering effects on you in the present.

It's easy to forget that a whole range of thoughts and emotions come with all our "busyness." They adversely affect us – physically, mentally, emotionally, and spiritually. Do you realize that each experience you have is recorded in every cell of your body? Even when you finally sink into bed, it's difficult to get a good rest because your body is still in overdrive.

More importantly, your body is weakened by the memory of stress – even though the effects may not show up for months or years. Many illnesses have root causes that began years before. It is definitely worth it to find and maintain balance for health, more positive relationships, and enjoyment of today!

It is possible to maintain centeredness and peacefulness and find *Balance in this Wobbly World*. Let's consider behaviors and tools you can use immediately to help you get the balance and joy back into your life.

Dr. Sheran Mattson ♡

You can practice the five Ps:

❋ **Plan**

❋ **Prioritize/Eliminate**

❋ **Play**

❋ **Positivity**

❋ **Pick Your Yeses**

This book offers simple methods to get you immediate results. You can start on any "P" but you may want to read all 5 first to decide which is best for you. Let's define the 5 Ps and I'll show you how you can *Maintain Balance in a Wobbly World*.

Get ready to find relief
&
achieve more joy and balance!

What Am I Balancing?

How do you create more balance, time, and joy? First you must acknowledge what's happening right now.

Since you are usually quite good at taking care of others, you may not be fully aware of all the roles you play. You started life with someone else taking care of you, but as the years unfolded, you took on more and more responsibility. Sometimes you did this because you enjoyed what you were doing, but other times you did so from a sense of obligation.

First let's figure out what taps your energy. Who and what are you supporting? Below is a list of possible roles you may have. Review the list and note which ones are true for you. Add others that may be missing.

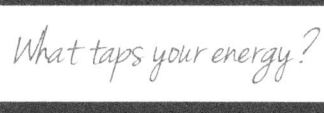

Maintaining Balance in a Wobbly World ♡

My Roles

(Check all roles that apply)

- ☐ Wife
- ☐ Mother
- ☐ Daughter
- ☐ Sister
- ☐ Aunt
- ☐ Grandmother
- ☐ Granddaughter
- ☐ Mother-in-Law
- ☐ Step-mother
- ☐ Step-daughter
- ☐ Sister-in-Law
- ☐ Employer
- ☐ Money Manager
- ☐ Employee
- ☐ Caregiver
- ☐ Single Parent
- ☐ Student
- ☐ Volunteer
- ☐ _____
- ☐ _____

Dr. Sheran Mattson ♡

- Husband ☐
- Father ☐
- Son ☐
- Brother ☐
- Uncle ☐
- Grandfather ☐
- Grandson ☐
- Father-in-Law ☐
- Step-father ☐
- Step-son ☐
- Brother-in-Law ☐
- Employer ☐
- Money Manager ☐
- Employee ☐
- Caregiver ☐
- Single Parent ☐
- Student ☐
- Volunteer ☐
- _____ ☐
- _____ ☐

Are you surprised by all you have chosen?

Each of these roles requires you to act in a certain way and take on activities that demand your attention and time. Whew! No wonder you feel out of balance!

But this is not your only challenge. Many of these roles have overlapping concerns that make it hard to prioritize. Let's take a closer look at the specific responsibilities you have. Don't despair – this is just to determine where you are. Later we'll discuss how to find relief!

My Responsibilities
(Check all that apply)

- ☐ Meal preparation
- ☐ Baking
- ☐ Menu planning
- ☐ Dishes
- ☐ Housecleaning
- ☐ Laundry
- ☐ Mending / clothing care
- ☐ Grocery shopping
- ☐ Yard work
- ☐ Home maintenance
- ☐ Decorating
- ☐ Entertaining
- ☐ Time with friends
- ☐ Care of children
- ☐ Care of parents
- ☐ Care of spouse
- ☐ Care of others
- ☐ Career / job tasks at work
- ☐ Career / job tasks at home
- ☐ Work / business travel

- ☐ Pleasure travel
- ☐ Special events planning
- ☐ Parent-Teacher meetings
- ☐ Doctor appointments
- ☐ Calendar scheduling
- ☐ Necessity phone calls
- ☐ Necessity shopping
- ☐ Trash collection / recycling
- ☐ Classes
- ☐ Homework / assignments
- ☐ Seminars for career / job
- ☐ Community involvement
- ☐ 1:1 with family members
- ☐ Letters / cards
- ☐ Pet care
- ☐ Plant care
- ☐ Car maintenance
- ☐ Carpooling
- ☐ Commute time
- ☐ Exercise / fitness
- ☐ Family outings
- ☐ Grooming
- ☐ Bathing
- ☐ Dressing
- ☐ Eating
- ☐ Sleeping
- ☐ Volunteer work
- ☐ Faith community
- ☐ Taxes
- ☐ Budgeting
- ☐ Bills
- ☐ Charity activities
- ☐ Sports activities
- ☐ Television
- ☐ Music
- ☐ Reading
- ☐ Cultural arts
- ☐ Hobbies
- ☐ Computer work / play
- ☐ Singing
- ☐ Dancing
- ☐ Movies
- ☐ Alone time
- ☐ _____
- ☐ _____
- ☐ _____

Is it any wonder you feel like this?

Take a moment to consider the options:

Activities I can reduce or give up:

_____
_____
_____
_____
_____

Activities I want to add to my ideal life:

_____
_____
_____
_____
_____

Once you've determined you want something to be different, it's time to consider how to get there!

Dr. Sheran Mattson ♡

There are many routes, and no definite path. You can start anywhere.

Sometimes one action has multiple results. You may need to practice just one of the Ps and that will be enough. Or you may want to do two or three. Only you can decide.

I promise you will find something to help in each of the 5 Ps. It's up to you to pick and choose which solutions appeal to you most and then decide if you want more!

Plan

End the Day Well

We often hear about the importance of planning, but we feel like failures when we're too overwhelmed to even begin. We make a list of tasks we fully intend to do, but feel guilty when we don't complete them all by the end of the day.

Do you try to cram too much into your day? Or do you have numerous interruptions? Unexpected things come up, over which you believe you have no control.

Your many roles may be in conflict, necessitating diverse demands all at once. There are children, spouses, bosses, or parents who are demanding attention! All of that is true, but you do not have to be a victim!

Prepare for life in the now

You have the choice to plan how you start and end each day.

How you end one day and how you begin the next are powerfully connected!

Getting enough sleep is critical for health, outlook, and also for handling "daily drama." Benefits of sleep include improved memory, enhanced immune system, more creativity, better attention span, weight control and reduced stress.

At least 6-8 hours are critical for being refreshed. A 2013 study from the National Academy of Sciences tells us that getting under 6 hours of sleep a night contributes to obesity, increased stress, reduced cognitive effectiveness, and may even shorten your life span.

> *You may need to sacrifice some activities in life, but **sleep** should not be one of them!*

Sleep helps you make better decisions and contributes to a more positive outlook. It may take a little rearranging to add sleep hours but it is critical.

Before bedtime, make a list of at least three things for which you are grateful. By keeping a written gratitude list, you will be able to appreciate how much good you have in spite of all the challenges. You may even want to post your gratitudes on Facebook or share them with significant others.

Gratitude multiplies. The more you appreciate, the more good things show up!

Use the checklist below to get started and then come up with lots more.

Make sure your sleeping space is inviting. You can spray lavender mist on the pillow and bed to increase the peacefulness.

I like to cuddle with a favorite pillow. This immediately signals to my brain that it is now time to move into a deeper level of consciousness. We go through stages from wakefulness to sleep. Just observe a baby to be reminded of your own process. There is the closing of eyes, stilling of the body, tuning out the noise around us, and eventually moving into a deeper realm.

As you fall asleep you want to state to yourself that you are going to be refreshed and wake up with a lot of energy. Your last thoughts are what your brain remembers and will focus on as you sleep!

Choosing to fall asleep with a smile on your face supports the flow of endorphins and allows for more pleasant dreaming. This is a critical first step!

Maintaining Balance in a Wobbly World ♡

Considerations for Gratitude

Keep a gratitude journal next to your bed where you can write down the three blessings that you want to ponder as you move into slumber:

Today I am grateful for:

My good health

Having a peaceful day

My walk in nature

Great meals

My job

My children

Spending time with a friend

Love of spouse/significant other

The hug of a grandchild

My car

The kindness of _____

Attending a fun event

The Sun's warmth as I walked

The Rain

Mending a broken relationship

Dr. Sheran Mattson ♡

The smile after helping at _____

Fresh Air

Freedom to speak out about _____

The great book I am reading

My paycheck

A clean house

The tree I sat under

The massage I had

The snuggle of my cat or dog

Losing a pound

Gaining a pound

Hearing from an old friend

My parents

My comfy bed

The warmth in the room

_____

Set Intentions

The next step for planning is to start each day with intentions for the flow of the day. Your thoughts create your reality, your world, and your future. Two people can have the same experience but view it and feel it completely differently. So before you think about all the practical things you plan to do each day, consider how you want to create your day.

> *Your thoughts create your reality, your world, and your future.*

What do you want to have happen and how do you want the day to manifest itself? You have more influence over this than you think.

Notice when you wake up with the thought that the day is going to be challenging and exhausting. What usually happens? The entire universe cooperates to create a day consisting of one challenge after another.

Your brain is an organ that does not know truth. It believes what you tell it and will allow you to experience what you expose it to. Consider when you watch a roller coaster ride in a thrilling movie. Does your heart race? Do you feel the adrenaline rush? Does it feel real? Your brain helps your body to enter the experience.

It is the same with intentions!

Your body also emits a frequency that interacts with everything and can attract or repel energy. It is valuable to use this ability intentionally rather than acting unconsciously.

Setting intentions is simple but there are specific guidelines to be really effective.

Do not say *hope*, *try*, *want*, *to be*, or *not*.

Saying "I hope to…" or "I will be…" or "I want to…" or "I will try…" or "I am not…" is not actually an intention that can be realized.

Are you going to be trying or hoping forever?

When you say, "I intend that I am <u>not feeling sick,</u>" you have not declared what you want, but what you don't want.

The universe and our brain hear only the "not." Instead, you should declare, "I intend I am in perfect health!"

Each morning it is valuable to set at least three intentions for how the day will unfold. Intentions can be for the day or an ongoing focus. You can always set more, but if you follow the formula below you can easily state your intentions before you even get out of bed.

Formula for Intending:

Start with:	I intend that I am _____.
State:	3 or 4 positive strong intentions.
End with:	So it is!

Examples:

I intend that I am in perfect health. So it is!

I intend that I completed 10 errands with perfect ease and within the time allotted. So it is!

I intend that I am relaxed and confident in my speaking presentation at work. So it is!

I intend that I have sold 10 cars by September 3. So it is!

I intend that the earth and the water are cleaned and healed! So it is!

✹ My Plans

_____

_____

_____

_____

_____

_____

_____

_____

_____

Prioritize

Your Space Supports You

When you are out of balance you have difficulty prioritizing how you use your time. You feel stuck and overwhelmed because there's too much to do.

Consider how much time is spent just taking care of "stuff." Over time, you collect mounds and mounds of it. Stuff you felt you needed to have, stuff you received as gifts, and stuff you inherited from someone or someplace else.

> Only give attention to what MATTERS.

What we tend to forget is that everything – every piece of furniture, every collectible, every piece of clothing – comes with responsibilities that consume our energy. Everything takes up space and needs to be dusted, cleaned, or moved around. Often we don't even notice how much stuff we own until we move homes or are forced through a life transition.

What you may not realize is that you are losing precious time and energy because of things that no longer matter.

> *Is each item in your space worth keeping?*

Get rid of anything that is outdated, you never liked, or evokes bad memories when you look at it. These things sap your energy. The clothes that don't fit, the doodads that need to be dusted, the art on the wall that reminds you of a broken relationship – all no longer serve you. They suck time and energy out of your life.

Real energetic cords of connection flow between you and any object that holds emotional residue. If the emotion is positive, you feel invigorated. But if the emotion is sadness, anger, or frustration, you feel a tug, pull, or leak of energy!

How can you find the time to do something new (like hiking, taking dance lessons, or playing with your children) when you have so many things to take care of?

Make room for the new by cleaning out the old. As you create space for something new to show up, the universe is happy to fill the vacuum!

Donate, discard, or give away anything you don't need, like, or feel delighted with. This allows you to do good for others while caring for yourself. Consider who may enjoy the things you are giving away. There may be items that another has always wanted. How great to make space and bring pleasure to a friend,

Dr. Sheran Mattson ♡

relative, or someone in need! By donating to a reputable charity, you are making a contribution that impacts another person's life.

The energy in your office, home, or garage will be lighter once you've done an inventory and only have supportive items in your space. You'll find yourself renewed. Everything you own gives off energy, so make sure the things around you are "loving" you!

Do an inventory of every room, drawer, and even the car. This can be done simply at first, just one place at a time. But notice how much freer and lighter you feel! You'll experience more free time since you're not dusting, ignoring, or walking around something. It will free you up to consider what's most important in life.

Use the checklist below to start prioritizing what you own!

Room Checklist

Begin by setting aside time for each room, including bathrooms and closets, even the hallway. You probably have items in each of these spaces you've just become accustomed to seeing without considering how they drain you. You can really clear your space if you include the garage and attic, but start with the rooms you visit regularly.

Before you enter the room, find three boxes or large bags, a marker, and some labels to use as you start your room clearing. Label one "donations," the second "trash," and the other "giveaway." The giveaway box will have items that may be given to different people, so make sure you label them immediately as you place things inside so you don't have to remember or re-sort later!

Put the name of the room at the top of the form so you can keep track. Walk around the room slowly and scan each wall and counter or furniture piece. Note anything that should be removed.

When you find something that no longer serves you, immediately determine what box it should go in. Don't spend a lot of time rationalizing.

Trust your inner guidance (that little internal nudge that asks, "Why am I keeping this?"). If you need help because something is too heavy or you don't have time to complete the process, write the item down and decide right away in which box the item will be placed.

Try to set aside enough time to do a complete room before moving on to another. This can be done more easily when you truly pay attention to your inner voice!

Make arrangements as soon as possible to complete the donations and giveaways. When done with a room, leave it and walk back in a few hours to notice how much better it feels. There will be a lighter mood in the room, and you will feel more peaceful.

If you still notice a tug or uncomfortable feeling, look around and ask yourself what's still there that's drawing you toward it or pushing you away. Being conscious in this way, you will be able to feel the energy.

Dr. Sheran Mattson ♡

_____ **Room**

Item	Trash	Donate	Give Away

When you are finished with each room, take a deep breath and thank the space for supporting you. You'll be able to relax more in the rooms that are cleared and you will feel less stress. Enjoy the difference!

Dr. Sheran Mattson ♡

Get Rid of Tolerations

Tolerations are tasks, unfinished actions, or irritations we don't address which allow them to nag at us. They may be small or large issues.

Often we decide something is not worth addressing or we'll get to it later. We just put up with it, but we don't realize we're unconsciously bothered by postponing the inevitable. We don't realize how much energy we're wasting to keeping that tiny but nagging item on our To Do list.

These energy leaks cause us to feel distracted. No matter how much we ignore them they are on our mind. [We have to *choose* to ignore something, which also costs us energy!]

Tolerations can be in relationships, work, behaviors, or simple irritations. *Get rid of tolerations!*

An example of a "toleration" is a leaky faucet that doesn't get repaired immediately. Every time you hear the drip or walk in the bathroom and see the drip, drip, drip you are distracted, even if just for a second. In the back of your mind, you think, "I need to get that fixed."

If you were to handle it immediately or make the appointment with the plumber instantly, you wouldn't have to think about it any further. There would not be nagging thoughts about one more thing to handle.

Review your tolerations to help you prioritize. Take care of things as they occur and you will have fewer things to do. When you immediately address issues rather than tolerate them, you'll be freer to handle the bigger concerns that need your attention.

Although it may seem like a time-consuming distraction, handling an issue immediately actually gives you more time. You can automatically delete it from the to-do list in your mind!

Personal irritations with people that aren't addressed take up precious "brain" space and emotional energy. It's so important to let people know what's bothering you. Don't assume anyone is a mind reader.

If someone is aggravating you on purpose, then it is a sign of a deeper problem in the relationship that needs to be addressed. The longer you put up with a toleration, the more challenging it will become.

You may find yourself reacting out of proportion to something like socks left on the floor. If you had just addressed this issue sooner, you could have come to an agreement regarding the behavior.

Dr. Sheran Mattson ♡

Use the worksheet below to review your life. This may take some time, but when you are done, you will know what you want to do next. You have solutions to everything that shows up, so trust yourself!

Any time something new comes up, handle it immediately. You will feel more confident and be better able to focus on what is most important – YOU!

Have more leisure and peace! Start today!

Maintaining Balance in a Wobbly World ♡

Review of Tolerations

(e.g. work, with others, with yourself – home, behaviors, car, clothes):

- ✓ **Name three little irritations in life that deplete your energy or rob your joy on a consistent basis.**

    (e.g. the traffic--try a new route even if it is longer!)

    _____

    _____

- ✓ **What are you tolerating in your home that you haven't even thought about addressing until now?**

    (e.g. dripping faucets, broken lighting fixtures, carpet stains, etc. Call for repairs!)

    _____

    _____

- ✓ **What worries clutter up your mind that you could let go of today?**

    (e.g. other people's negative opinions of you. It is about them, not you!)

    _____

    _____

    _____

Dr. Sheran Mattson ♡

- ✓ **What are you putting up with in relationships? Name any conflicts, boundary issues, or problem situations that you're coping with instead of resolving.**

  (e.g. no follow-through on promises. Speak up or get an appointment with someone who can assist you with how to address the issue!)

  _____

  _____

  _____

- ✓ **What are the little quirks in your relationships that trigger reactions over and over? What are your quirks that bother your friends?**

  (e.g. remember why you chose to be friends in the first place and determine if these quirks are as important as why you became friends. Either discuss or accept them as part of the friendship!)

  _____

  _____

  _____

Maintaining Balance in a Wobbly World ♡

1 Prioritize/Eliminate

Play

Creative Social Activity

Enjoy an activity with pleasure, relaxation, and no obligation.

It's a proven fact that children learn and develop through play. The importance of play for adults is often dismissed as a waste of time or frivolous, when actually the opposite is true. Play contributes to better sleep, wellness, creativity, and reduced stress. Endorphins are released in the brain. Valuable chemicals soar through the body. This helps you keep balance and have a more positive outlook.

You need play as much as you need nutrition and exercise for your body and mind to work well and heal. Just as children learn through play, so do adults.

Here are some reasons you may want to play:

- to create
- to learn
- to feel challenged
- to pass time
- to calm and focus yourself
- as a spectator watching others
- competition
- cooperation
- for the fun of it
- for the joy of it

Play can connect you with others. Through play you socialize, enjoy friends, coworkers and your spouse as you see them in a new light. You can try on behaviors. Your children see you as a full human being and your activity validates their play!

Psychiatrist and writer Mihaly Csikszentmihalyi describes play as a flow state. Play is best when it has the balance of challenge and opportunity.

Dr. Sheran Mattson ♡

Feelings We Experience in the Flow State[1]

Involvement

Complete focus and concentration, either due to innate curiosity or as the result of training.

Delight

A sense of bliss and positive detachment from everyday reality.

Clarity

Great inner clarity and a built-in understanding about the state of affairs.

Confidence

An innate sense that the activity is doable and that your skills are adequate to the task. Additionally, you don't feel anxious or bored.

Serenity

A sense of peace and an absence of worry about self.

Timeliness

Thorough focus on the present and a lack of attention to the passing of time.

Motivation

Intrinsic understanding about what needs to be done and a desire to keep the moment of play moving.

---

[1] Kemp, G.., Smith, M., DeKoven, B., and Segal, J. (2012). Play, Creativity, and Lifelong Learning: Why Play Matters for Both Kids and Adults.
http://www.helpguide.org/life/creative_play_fun_games.htm

Social Activity

Fill in for each area below and see how much fun you can have!

A play activity I do TO BE CREATIVE

_____

A play activity I do WITH FRIENDS

_____

A play activity I do AS A SPECTATOR

_____

A play activity I do WITH FAMILY

_____

A play activity I do TO COMPETE

_____

Dr. Sheran Mattson ♡

A play activity I do FOR ACCOMPLISHMENT

_____

                          A play activity I do TO BE PHYSICALLY FIT

                          _____

A play activity I do that HELPS ME LAUGH

_____

A play activity I do TO HELP OTHERS

_____

A leisure activity I do TO BE MENTALLY STIMULATED

_____

A leisure activity I do TO LEARN SOMETHING NEW

_____

Alone Time

The other part of Play is **Alone Time.** Taking time to appreciate who you are is valuable for supporting yourself and others. It is an important part of self-care. Alone time does not equate with loneliness and it is not the same for each person. All alone time does involve unplugging from all technology, connecting with the inner self, and listening to the world around you. If you haven't done this for quite some time, it can seem daunting! But it truly is simple.

The world in which you live is constantly bombarding you with messages and stimulation. The messages are often so subtle that you don't even hear them as unique or recognize how they influence you. Media messages tell you what it means to be an effective parent, boss, or man or woman of today. All the "shoulds" show up! You begin comparing yourself to others. You wonder why you aren't as good or as accomplished or … or… or… ! You can never be enough to satisfy your critical self. In reality, you have no idea about the truth of another's journey, so there is no point in comparison.

Each person is unique and has her/his own perfect way of being. Only *you* can know what is appropriate for you. If you do not take time to reflect on this and make space to listen to the inner self, you may forget how to listen. This practice requires attention. For some, sitting in a quiet space for a few minutes each day is best. Others will want to walk or hike in nature. You could take a luxurious, long bath with silence and candles. Journaling for 15 minutes each day is another possibility. Whatever gives you a few minutes of alone time is what is important.

Dr. Sheran Mattson ♡

Some people value getting up 15-30 minutes early each day and others like to have a half hour alone after everyone is in bed. The important point is that this is sacred time that you honor to renew, enjoy, and appreciate yourself!

Here is a list of suggestions for alone time and you will come up with more:

- ♥ Journal for 10 minutes on anything
- ♥ A walk
- ♥ A hike
- ♥ A visit to a Farmer's Market
- ♥ Listen to music and dance by yourself
- ♥ Daydream for 10 minutes
- ♥ Draw
- ♥ A bath with candles
- ♥ Play with your pet for an extended time
- ♥ Make a fun meal just for yourself
- ♥ Go to a museum-with no one else
- ♥ Meditate
- ♥ Practice Tai Chi or Yoga alone
- ♥ Visit the library
- ♥ A movie by yourself
- ♥ Do a puzzle with numerous pieces

Maintaining Balance in a Wobbly World ♡

My Play

Positivity

Eliminate Negative Beliefs from the Past

Supportive and encouraging thoughts and language

Our behavior and actions are based on our thoughts. We first have a thought and then the action results. We often act based on habits or long forgotten events. Do you ever wonder why you repeat something you don't like or you hear yourself speaking like your parent… when you vowed you would never do that?

Much of the stress imbalance you experience is rooted in the Writing on Your Wall (other's opinions that you internalized as you grew up) which have created *negative self-limiting beliefs.*

Life provides many opportunities for disappointments, hurts, and discouragements that contribute to limiting beliefs. In childhood you may have been treated badly by peers, had a parent with unachievable standards, been embarrassed by a teacher, or not gotten invited to the prom! The list is endless and may even seem silly at this point in life. But each time you have a negative experience, your whole body and mind undergoes a disturbance that creates a negative self-limiting beliefs.

This interference does not disappear simply because you decide to have a happy thought. Of course the happy thought helps, but the negative is still there, buried beneath current thoughts. Your brain is an amazing storage vault. Much of what the brain does is protect us, but it doesn't know what's needed for future protection – or what can be discarded. It stores everything in case we need it again, such as to flee from a lion (as prehistoric people did) or to avoid public speaking because of one bad experience!

Your body condition is also affected by these disturbances. You feel stress and get off-balance easily when an old negative belief/emotion is triggered. In fact an ache, pain, or illness related to a negative emotion may take years to show up. The deeply embedded unreleased emotion works slowly behind the scenes and years later manifests in the physical body. Mind and body are closely connected. Even inherited conditions have an associated thought pattern.

The more you can identify and clean out unneeded negative emotions of the past, current self-limiting beliefs, and quickly deal with new negative experiences the better you will feel and more balance you will achieve in all areas of your life. You can do this with a little attention and effort. It is worth it!!

A simple but powerful practice can assist. Emotional Freedom Technique is so simple many people want to dismiss it! The wonderful fact is that one does not need to believe it to use it. Here is the basic outline that you can use immediately. Used on a regular basis you will experience greater peace and balance no matter what's going on around you. (More information at www.sheranmattson.com)

Dr. Sheran Mattson ♡

EFT Protocol

Use this mind body technique to get quick results. It looks funny but works powerfully when followed accurately!

Think of a negative experience. Recall it in as much detail as possible. Recognize the emotion you feel right now as you think of the experience. Rate how strong you feel it from 1-10, with 1 being low and 10 being very strong. Write the number down so you can note the change that happens. Think about words to describe the experience and then follow the outline below to tap on acupressure points while making simple statements that keep you focused on the experience.

Begin by tapping on the Karate Chop point (on the side of your hand) and repeat the following statement **twice.**

> **Even though I have**_____
> (this experience and describe what you think)
>
> **and I feel it in my body as** _____
> (e.g. a knot in my stomach, pain in my heart),
>
> **I deeply and completely accept myself.**

Tap on each acupressure point about 7 times using your fingers from one hand. It does not matter which side you tap or which hand you use. State some aspect of the story as you tap. You do not need to say a sentence, just a phrase while tapping on the points. The phrase just keeps you centered in the feeling as you may want to drift to another thought. It is very important to stay with this one experience.

When finished tapping on all the points, take a deep breath and rate the intensity of the emotion from 1-10. If you are not at 0, do the tapping again. If a new thought comes up, write it down, but finish with the current negative experience and only do the new one after the first emotion is at 0.

If you get stuck, *then add the words:*

> **"Even though I still have this memory of**
> (experience)
>
> **I deeply and completely accept myself."**
>
> Do the process again and assess.
> You want to get as close to 0 as possible.

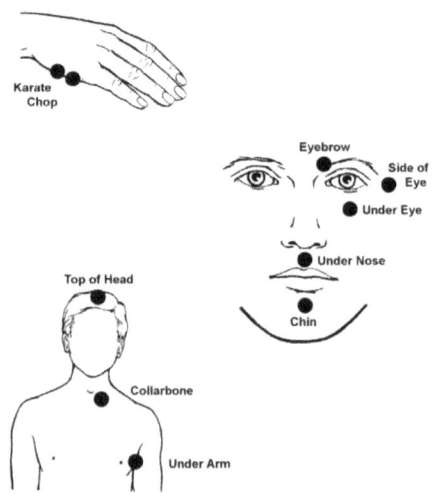

Dr. Sheran Mattson ♡

An example of the process is:

Tap on KC Repeat 2 times	Say: Even though I remember my mother yelling at me when I came home from school with a D on my report card and it makes me short of breath, I deeply and completely accept myself.
Top Head	Say: shortness of breath
Eyebrow	Say: shortness of breath
Side of Eye	Say: shortness of breath
Under Eye	Say: shortness of breath
Under Nose	Say: D on report card
Chin Point	Say: shortness of breath
Collarbone	Say: D on report card
Under Arm	Say: D on report card

This simple tapping exercise, when done accurately, will release disruption that blocked your system in relation to the episode you chose to tap on.

You may want to make a list of as many experiences that you can remember and tap on each. Use this to tap on anything that comes up in the present and future, also.

(If you feel the need, you may want to do this with a partner. This information does not take the place of any medical or psychological advice and is for self-care only!)

For more information
Visit www.emofree.com

Surround Yourself with Positivity

The world in which we live does not support positive thinking. The media likes to report negative news since there is a belief that negative stories sell better. These are the ones that get the headlines in news broadcasts whether in print, Internet, or on television. We are bombarded with stories of loss, pain, and abuse! Much of the entertainment we view also focuses on the negative side of human nature.

Marketing campaigns to encourage us to purchase products make a point of telling us we are not attractive enough, thin enough, or smart enough. Your home, your vehicle, and your wardrobe continually need to be updated or you will not "fit in" or "stand out." All of this often happens without us questioning the value of the messages we receive.

Is it any wonder you feel off balance? It is impossible to keep up with ever-changing standards of acceptance.

To support your goal of balance, *surround yourself with positivity.*

This requires a commitment to become conscious of what you look at and listen to, as well as how you speak and think. How important is it to watch nightly news or listen to the latest gossip about a celebrity? How often do you hear and/or spread gossip about friends or family members?

Probably of all the methods to maintaining balance in a wobbly world, this is the most challenging. The habits of negativity are deeply rooted in our experience. It also takes courage not to participate in negativity and to excuse ourselves from being around people and places that are negative.

When making a commitment to positivity, it is best to start noticing language and thoughts. A first step is to focus for 15-30 minutes on every thought you think or word you speak to filter out or reframe any negativity.

This may seem a short time, but you will be surprised how much goes on unconsciously in your head. For example: "It sure is really hot or cold." "There I go again forgetting to...." "Why is this traffic so slow?" "I never get that to work right." "She sure looks funny in that outfit." You could add more to the list and some of these don't even seem like complaining or negativity, but they are.

Now let's consider an example of how to reframe each of these statements to be more positive. Some of these may be silly, but it will help you practice being more positive. Sincerity is important, but the old adage "Fake it until you make it" is also helpful to remember.

"It sure is really hot or cold."	"Another day of sunshine or another day of being able to wear my warm coat."
"There I go again forgetting to...."	"I'm so glad I noticed I had to do this."
"Why is this traffic so slow?"	"This is a good time for me to take some deep breaths or listen to my favorite CD."
"I never get that to work."	"I am going to ask Joe to help me learn this – he has it figured out."
"She sure looks funny in that outfit."	"Jane sure is creative and comfortable in her dress style."

To develop positivity, you can reframe negative thoughts, make conscious choices about what you expose yourself to, and excuse yourself from gossip and negative conversations. You will be surprised how much more balanced you feel!

My Positivity

Pick Your Yeses

Say No Without Guilt

Be assertive in choosing actions that support your highest self

As already noted, there are many roles you manage in your daily life. You are often asked to respond to numerous demands. The asker may truly need help. Individually each request may seem reasonable and you may feel obligated because of your "role."

If you find yourself exhausted, out of balance, or resentful, you need to stop and ask yourself if the *yes* you say is the only answer possible.

How often do you say yes out of obligation without taking time to determine if you want to say yes… if you are the most appropriate person to say yes… or if your personal needs and wants will be ignored if you say yes?

You have a right and responsibility to *say no without guilt* when you determine it to be in your best interest.

If you're feeling overwhelmed or resentful by all you've committed to do, you have to ask yourself some difficult questions. Are you actually being selfish? Are you focusing on a sense of pride or exhibiting a sense of control? These can be unconscious actions. You need to take time before you commit to a "yes" that's going to rob you of peace of mind or balance.

You can consider a request before responding. Silently ask yourself some questions. Based on the answers you get, you can determine if yes or no is the best response!

Sample questions to ask are:

- ♡ Do I really want to do this?
- ♡ If it has to be done, is there someone else who could do it (maybe even better than me)?
- ♡ Does this fit in with my values and goals?
- ♡ Will this action be energizing to me and/or the other person?

It is most important to determine your real intention and then measure your answers against that intention. Saying yes without thinking about the consequences to health and wellbeing can be a habit. Habits are sometimes hard to break, and if we start saying "no" we may disappoint others. The first "no" is the hardest. But with practice you'll get better, and you'll actually find yourself being appreciated more for the times you do say yes.

The most important part of practicing this new habit is to do so without guilt or regrets, no matter how another may respond. If you've honestly determined you should say no to an activity – the activity is either unnecessary, could be done better by someone else, or could be delayed without harm to anyone – then you are acting with integrity!

You'll be teaching both yourself and others how to appreciate you. When you do say yes, you will feel satisfied and complete!

Dr. Sheran Mattson ♡

Your health and peace of mind will be reflected in your attitude and actions! Balance and less stress is a great byproduct!

Choose Energizing Actions

When you feel out of balance in this wobbly world, you are brought back to balance by *choosing energizing actions* that make a difference in the world at large. By doing something that supports your goals and makes an impact in the world, you recognize your life has purpose and meaning. The action(s) you choose can be simple but far reaching in effect.

Choose from the following: "64 Ways in 64 Days" from the Gandhi Institute for Nonviolence, Mile HI Church of Religious Science, Regis University, 7 News. (Used by permission)

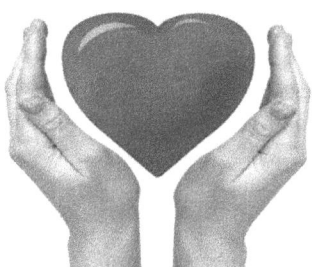

1. Today, I will reflect on what peace means to me.
2. Today, I will look for opportunities to be a peacemaker.
3. Today, I will practice nonviolence and respect for Mother Earth by making good use of her resources.
4. Today, I will take time to admire and appreciate nature.
5. Today, I will plant seeds or constructive ideas.

6. Today, I will hold a vision of plenty for all the world's hungry and be open to guidance as to how I can help alleviate some of that hunger.
7. Today, I will acknowledge every human being's fundamental right to justice, equity and equality.
8. Today, I will appreciate the earth's bounty and all those who work to make my food available (i.e. grower, trucker, grocery clerk, cook, waitress, etc.)
9. Today, I will work to understand and respect another culture.
10. Today, I will oppose injustice, not people.
11. Today, I will look beyond stereotypes and prejudices.
12. Today I will choose to be aware of what I talk about and I will refuse to gossip.
13. Today I will live in the present moment and release the past.
14. Today, I will silently acknowledge all the leaders throughout the world.

---

15. Today, I will speak with kindness, respect, and patience to every person I talk with..

---

16. Today, I will affirm my value and worth with positive "self-talk" and refuse to put myself down.
17. Today, I will tell the truth and speak honestly from the heart.
18. Today, I will cause a ripple effect of good by an act of kindness toward another.
19. Today, I will choose to use my talents to serve others by volunteering a portion of my time.
20. Today I will say a blessing for greater understanding whenever I see evidence of crime, vandalism, or graffiti.
21. Today, I will say "NO" to ideas and actions that violate me or others.

Dr. Sheran Mattson ♡

22. Today, I will turn off anything that portrays or supports violence whether on television, in the movie or on the Internet.
23. Today, I will greet this day – everyone and everything – with openness and acceptance as if I were encountering them for the first time.
24. Today, I will drive with tolerance and patience.
25. Today, I will constructively channel my anger, frustration or jealousy into healthy physical activities (i.e. doing sit-ups, picking up trash, taking a walk).
26. Today, I will take time to appreciate the people who provide me with challenges in my life, especially those who make me angry or frustrated.
27. Today, I will talk less and listen more.
28. Today, I will notice the peacefulness in the world around me.
29. Today, I will recognize that my actions directly affect others.
30. Today, I will take time to tell a family member or friend how much they mean to me.
31. Today I will acknowledge and thank someone for acting kindly.
32. Today, I will send a kind anonymous message to someone.
33. Today, I will identify something special in everyone I meet.
34. Today, I will discuss ideas about nonviolence with a friend to gain new perspectives.
35. Today, I will practice praise rather than criticism.
36. Today, I will strive to learn from my mistakes.
37. Today, I will tell at least one person that they are special & important.
38. Today, I will hold children tenderly in thought and/or action.
39. Today, I will listen without defending and speak without judgment.
40. Today I will help someone in trouble.
41. Today, I will listen with an open heart to at least one person.

42. Today, I will treat the elderly I encounter with respect and dignity.
43. Today, I will treat the children I encounter with respect and care, knowing that I serve as a model to them.
44. Today, I will see my co-workers in a new light with understanding and compassion.
45. Today, I will be open to other ways of thinking and acting that are different from my own.
46. Today, I will think of at least three alternative ways I can handle a situation when confronted with conflict.
47. Today, I will work to help others resolve differences.
48. Today, I will express my feelings honestly and nonviolently with respect for myself and others.
49. Today, I will sit down with my family for one meal.
50. Today, I will set an example of a peacemaker by promoting nonviolent responses.
51. Today, I will use no violent language.
52. Today, I will pause for reflection.
53. Today, I will hold no one hostage to the past, seeing each as I see myself as a work in progress.
54. Today, I will make a conscious effort to smile at someone whom I have held a grudge against in the past.
55. Today, I will practice compassion and forgiveness by apologizing to someone whom I have hurt in the past.
56. Today, I will reflect on whom I need to forgive and take at least one step in that direction.

57. Today, I will forgive myself.

58. Today, I will embrace the spiritual belief of my heart in my own personal and reflective way.

59. Today, I will enlarge my capacity to embrace differences and appreciate the value of every human being.
60. Today, I will be compassionate in my thought, words and actions.
61. Today, I will cultivate my moral strength and courage through education and creative nonviolent actions.
62. Today, I will practice compassion and forgiveness for myself and others.
63. Today, I will use my talents to serve others as well as myself.
64. Today, I will serve humanity by dedicating myself to a vision greater than myself.

❈ My Yeses

_____

_____

_____

_____

_____

_____

_____

_____

_____

Final Thoughts

Maintaining *Balance in a Wobbly World* is possible. The most important thing of all is to LOVE YOURSELF. It is possible to practice any of the 5 Ps at any time. Life is better when it is balanced.

 Plan

 Prioritize/Eliminate

 Play

 Positivity

 Pick Your Yeses

Working with a Coach

Working with a coach is a great way to stay focused and leap forward. Additional workshops and one-on-one support is available for any and all 5 Ps and much more. Visit www.sheranmattson.com for information or contact me at sheran@dynamiclifecoach.net to support your *Balance in this Wobbly World*.

www.ingramcontent.com/pod-product-compliance
Lightning Source LLC
Chambersburg PA
CBHW071636040426
42452CB00009B/1659